Independent Order of. Petaluma Odd Fellows, J. A Cowen

Constitution, By-Laws and Rules of Order of Petaluma Lodge,

No. 30

Of the Independent Order of Odd Fellows of the State of California

Independent Order of. Petaluma Odd Fellows, J. A Cowen

Constitution, By-Laws and Rules of Order of Petaluma Lodge, No. 30
Of the Independent Order of Odd Fellows of the State of California

ISBN/EAN: 9783337157906

Printed in Europe, USA, Canada, Australia, Japan

Cover: Foto ©Suzi / pixelio.de

More available books at **www.hansebooks.com**

CONSTITUTION,

BY-LAWS AND RULES OF ORDER

—OF—

Petaluma Lodge, No. 30,

—OF THE—

Independent Order of Odd Fellows

—OF THE—

STATE OF CALIFORNIA.

———※———

INSTITUTED SEPTEMBER 30th, 1854

———※———

JOS. A. COWEN, BOOKBINDER & PRINTER, PETALUMA.

CONSTITUTION

—OF—

Petaluma Lodge No. 30.

I. O. O. F.

+>◇<+

PREAMBLE.

For the purpose of effecting uniformity in the administration of the privileges, honors and benefits of Odd Fellowship within this jurisdiction, the GRAND LODGE OF THE INDEPENDENT ORDER OF ODD FELLOWS OF THE STATE OF CALIFORNIA ordains the following Constitution of Subordinate Lodges under its jurisdiction. •

ARTICLE I.

NAME.

SECTION 1. This Lodge shall consist of at least five members of the Degree of Truth, including one qualified to preside at its meetings, to be hailed and entitled

PETALUMA LODGE, No. 30

of the Independent Order of Odd Fellows of California, holding a legal charter granted by the

Grand Lodge of the Independent Order of Odd Fellows of the State of California. It cannot voluntarily surrender its charter so long as five Third-degree members in good standing object thereto.

ARTICLE II.

MEMBERSHIP.

SECTION 1. Every applicant for initiation must be a free white male of the age of twenty-cne years; of sound health; of good moral character and industrious habits, having some known respectable means of support; must believe in the existence of a Supreme Being, the Creator and Preserver of the Universe, ard be proposed in the Lodge nearest his residence, except that Lodge grant permission for his joining another Lodge; *provided*, that application for membership may be made to any Lodge nearest the residence of the applicant in the same county or district. A candidate may be admitted in any Lodge in the city or village in which he resides; but all candidates for initiation must reside in this jurisdiction, except such candidates as may apply from other States or Territories where there is no Grand Lodge or District Deputy Grand Sire located.

SEC. 2. Every applicant for membership by deposit of card, or certificate of dismissal, or as an Ancient Odd Fellow, shall deposit his card or certificate with his proposition, or furnish satisfactory evidence that such card or certificate has been lost.

Sec. 3. No suspended or expelled member of the Order can be admitted to membership in this Lodge except on a dismissal certificate or on being reinstated and receiving a withdrawal card from the Lodge which suspended or expelled him, or from the Grand Secretary, as prescribed by law.

Sec. 4. An Odd Fellow who has been regularly initiated into the Order, and has retained membership therein for at least five consecutive years, and who at the time of making application for reinstatement or membership shall be over fifty years of age, may be admitted to membership in this Lodge as a non-beneficial member upon such terms as the By-Laws may prescribe, by presenting a petition as required under Section 1, Article III, for proposals for membership by initiation, which shall be disposed of according to said section.

Sec 5. When an application for membership is received from a person residing nearer to another Lodge than the one to which the application is made, the Lodge receiving such application shall communicate the fact to the Lodge nearest the residence of such applicant, and shall inquire whether such person is a fit and proper person to be admitted into our Order, and, if in the same county and district, shall also ask the consent of such Lodge to receive and act upon such application; and it shall take no further action upon such application until an answer is received to such communication. The Lodge receiving such communication shall appoint a committee of three to investigate the character, standing and health of the petitioner, in the same manner as if the application was made directly to such Lodge. Such committee shall report at the next regular meeting of the Lodge, and a certified copy of the report, together with a certified copy of the minutes show'ng the action of the Lodge, upon the request for consent to receive and act upon the application (if such consent was necessary), shall be forthwith forwarded to the Lodge in which such application is filed, and said last named Lodge may then proceed upon such application as in other cases, except that if it be a case where the consent of the other Lodge is necessary, and that consent be refused, the petitioner's money (if any has been paid) shall be returned, and no further action shall be had in the premises.

ARTICLE III.

PROPOSITIONS FOR MEMBERSHIP.

Section i. The name of a person offered for membership, with his age, nativity, residence and occupation must be proposed by a member in writing, signed by the applicant, with the names of two persons as references attached, and entered upon the record, and forthwith be referred to a committee of three members for investigation, who shall report at the next succeeding regular meeting (unless extraordinary circumstances prevent), when the candidate shall be balloted for with ball ballots, and if three or more black balls appear, the candidate shall be declared rejected.

SEC. 2. A brother who has been for twenty-five years a contributing member of a Subordinate Lodge, who may desire to join this Lodge by deposit of card, may make application for admission before severing his connection with this Lodge by sending in his petition setting forth the fact of his having been a member for that length of time, together with such other matter as is usually contained in petitions for membership; whereupon the Lodge shall proceed to consider such application in the usual manner, and in case of the election of such applicant, the Secretary shall immediately notify the Lodge to which the brother belongs, and when the brother's withdrawal card shall have been received by the Secretary of this Lodge, and he has paid the admission fee, he shall be entitled to sign the Constitution, and thereby be received into full membership.

SEC. 3. Should this Lodge receive notification that one of its members has been so elected to membership by another Lodge, this Lodge shall, at the meeting when such notification is received, grant such brother a withdrawal card—if he is clear on the books of the Lodge and free from all charges—upon the payment of the requisite fee, and the Secretary shall immediately forward the card to the Lodge from which the notification of the brother's election to membership comes.

SEC. 4. No reconsideration of an unfavorable ballot can be had unless all the brothers who may cast black balls against an applicant for membership voluntarily make a motion for a reconsideration of the ballot ; *provided* such reconsideration be had within four regular meeting nights next succeeding such rejection ; and in such case the vote on the reconsideration shall be taken by ball ballots, and if all the balls cast be in favor of it, the reconsideration shall be had ; whereupon the application shall lie over till the succeeding meeting, when another ballot shall be had with ball ballots, and if the same be unanimously in favor of the applicant he shall thereby be elected ; but if one or more black balls appear in either ballot, the applicant shall be rejected ; and in no case shall a reconsideration be had except upon a voluntary motion of all those who cast black balls ; and never more than one motion for a reconsideration in the same case shall be allowed. A favorable balloting can be reconsidered at any meeting prior to the admission of the candidate, *provided* a majority of the members present agree thereto.

SEC. 5. When a candidate for initiation has been rejected, notice thereof shall be sent, without delay, to the Grand Secretary, and to all the Lodges in the county and district, and he cannot be proposed again in any Lodge for the space of one year after such rejection. All other applications for membership may be renewed at any time.

SEC. 6. No proposition can be withdrawn after being referred to a committee, unless by consent of two-thirds of the members present at a regular meeting, and before the report of the committee has been read to the Lodge.

SEC. 7. If any person shall gain admittance to any Lodge upon a petition containing any false representations, he shall be expelled.

SEC. 8 In case the name of any member of the Order shall at any time appear—upon memorial duly presented by him—not to be his correct name, the Lodge may, upon motion duly made therefor, order such name changed upon the records of the Lodge to his true name ; provided a motion therefor shall be submitted in writing at least two weeks prior to action thereon ; and provided further that two-thirds of the members present at the meeting of the Lodge consent thereto, and the Secretary shall report such action to the Grand Secretary, who shall report the same to all the Lodges in the jurisdiction.

ARTICLE IV.

FEES, DUES AND BENEFITS.

SECTION 1. The fees of this Lodge shall not be less than $10 for initiation; $5 for each degree; $5 for admission by card; $8 for an Ancient Odd Fellow, and $10 by deposit of Dismissal Certificate. The dues of this Lodge shall not be less than fifty cents per month. In addition to the foregoing, the Lodge may provide by its By-Laws for a Widows', Orphans' and Education Fund, and Funeral Tax, and for extraordinary assessments for Lodge purposes.

SEC. 2. Every member qualified as required by the By-Laws shall, in case of being disabled by sickness or bodily accident from earning a livelihood, be entitled to and may receive such weekly benefits as may be fixed by law from the funds of the Lodge, which shall in no case be less than four dollars per week for Third-degree members; but the Lodge may provide in its By-Laws that none but Third-degree members shall be entitled to weekly benefits; also that benefits shall not be allowed for the first week's sickness. Such benefits shall commence six months from the date of admission to membership, *provided* the brother shall have attained the degree required by the By-Laws; and all brothers, if otherwise qualified, shall be entitled to benefits if not more than thirteen weeks in arrears for dues, assessments or fines. Benefits are rights personal to the member, his family and dependent relatives, and are not payable to the legal representatives of a member's estate.

SEC. 3. In case of the death of a member, irrespective of his standing relative to sick benefits, there shall be allowed from the Lodge a uniform sum of not less than thirty dollars to defray the expenses of the burial, to be paid by the Noble Grand on account of the funeral; *provided* the brother be buried by the Order or at the expense of the family of the deceased. In the absence of competent relations, the Noble Grand shall take charge of the funeral and render an account of the disbursements. In addition to the above, the Lodge may provide in its By-Laws for a funeral benefit.

SEC. 4. The funeral and sick benefits shall be regulated by the By-Laws of the Lodge, and all orders drawn for the above benefits shall be by vote of the Lodge.

SEC. 5. If a Lodge refuses or neglects to grant sick benefits to a brother, he may, at any time within four weeks thereafter, demand in writing, that the Lodge appoint a committee to investigate the matter, whereupon the Lodge shall appoint a committee of five to hear the evidence and report the facts and their conclusions to the Lodge. Such committee shall, without unnecessary delay, notify the brother of the time and place of their meeting,

and investigate the case. They shall keep full
minutes of the evidence and of their proceedings,
and report the same to the Lodge with their conclusion. If a witness be a member of the Order, he
shall give his testimony on the honor of an Odd
Fellow; if he be not a member, then on oath or
affirmation, and the proceedings must state that
such obligation or oath was administered. The
obligation may be administered by any member of
the committee. No testimony shall be taken without notice or opportunity for cross-examination by
the opposing party. Upon the report being made,
notice thereof shall forthwith be given by the Secretary to the party against whom the verdict is
rendered, and he shall have two weeks in which to
file his exceptions; if no exceptions are filed within two weeks, the Lodge shall proceed to pronounce
its judgment and decision. An appeal from the
judgment of the Lodge may be taken at any time
within two weeks thereafter to the Grand Lodge on
questions of law, of fact, or both, and if no such
appeal is taken, the judgment of the Lodge is final.
When a Bill of Exceptions to the report of the
committee is filed, as above provided, the Lodge
may determine upon its merits, and either change,
modify or sustain the report of the committee, or
refer the same back to the same, or another committee, or order a new investigation. If the Lodge
shall deem the exceptions not well taken, it shal

proceed to pronounce its judgment and decision. Each witness, at the conclusion of his testimony, and before other proceedings in the case are had, shall have his testimony, as taken down by the committee, read over to him, and shall make such corrections thereof as he may deem proper, and shall thereupon sign each page of said testimony. The brother has the affirmative of the issue ; and the committees appointed under this section shall be appointed and governed by the rules applicable to committees upon trials under charges.

SFC. 6 This Constitution and all laws, rules and regulations providing for the granting of sick, funeral and other benefits, or of any aid, relief, assistance, allowance, expenses, or money to any member, wife, widow, orphan, or any person whatever, or providing for the payment to the Lodge of dues, assessments and demands by a member, are not intended and shall not be construed to create the relation of debtor and creditor, nor to create legal rights, liabilities nor responsibilities, nor any legal contracted relation, nor confer any right to enforce the granting or payment of the same by resort to courts of law ; on the contrary, all questions, whether of law or fact, relative to the granting, payment or refusal of the same, relate to moral duties or obligations, and not to legal ones, and appertain to the sole jurisdiction of this Lodge and the authorities of this Order, and their decisions in the premises shall be binding, corclusive, and final upon all members, wives, widows, orphans or persons. Every person by becoming or continuing a member of this Lodge consents to and agrees to abide by all the laws and decisions of this Lodge and of the authorities of the Order.

SEC. 7. The Constitution, Laws and Decisions of the Sovereign Grand Lodge of the Independent Order of Odd Fellows, and the Constitution, Laws and Decisions of the Grand Lodge of the Independent Order of Odd Fellows of the State of California, are laws of this Lodge, and all persons, by becoming or continuing members of this Lodge, consent to, and agree to abide by the same.

SEC 8. No benefits shall be paid for any injury or disability received in the commission of a crime or an immoral act, nor for any sickness or disability arising from any criminal or immoral acts, conduct, causes or considerations, nor in cases where the same contribute thereto. No benefit or allowance shall be paid to any widow of an Odd Fellow except while she maintains a good moral character in fact, and in case a Lodge neglects or refuses to grant the same on account of any immoral act or conduct, or otherwise, she may demand within four weeks thereafter the appointment of a committee, as provided in Section 5 of this Article, and said Section shall, in all matters, including manner and time of appeal, be applicable thereto In cases where the Lodge refuses or neglects to pay any benefit or relief, or allowance, which our laws provide shall be paid, the person may, within four weeks thereafter, likewise demand a committee, as provided in said Section 5, and the Section shall likewise, in all matters, including the time and manner of appeal, be applicable thereto.

ARTICLE V.
DEGREES.

SECTION 1. Application for election to either of the three subordinate degrees shall be accompanied with the amount required therefor, and presented to the Lodge, under the proper head, when the Lodge shall ballot upon the application, and if not more than two black balls or cubes be cast, he shall be declared elected ; and if the Lodge does not confer the degrees upon its own members, a certificate shall be given the applicant, addressed to a Degree Lodge, or officer authorized to confer degrees, showing that he is a member of this Lodge, and has been authorized to receive them.

SEC. 2. Not more than one degree shall be conferred upon a candidate at any one meeting, except by dispensation. If any degree be refused a brother, no application shall be again received from him within three months.

ARTICLE VI.
OFFICERS.

SECTION 1. The elective officers shall consist of

a Noble Grand, Vice Grand, Secretary and Treasurer, who shall serve a regular term each, *provided* that the Treasurer may be elected for the period of one year ; and the Lodge may also elect a Permanent Secretary and three Trustees; *provided*, that no member shall hold any two of said offices at the same time.

SEC. 2. The appointed officers shall consist of a Warden, Conductor, Outside Guardian, Inside Guardian, Right Supporter to Noble Grand, Left Supporter to Noble Grand, Right Supporter to Vice-Grand, Left supporter to Vice-Grand, and Right and Left Scene Supporters, who shall each serve a regular term, and the Lodge may also appoint·a Chaplain for a regular term.

SEC. 3. No member of this Lodge shall be installed as Noble Grand unless he has served a term as Vice-Grand, or the last of a term to fill a vacancy ; or as Vice-Grand, unless he has served twenty-six weeks in an inferior office other than Trustee or Chaplain. Service in office, whether elective or appointed, is qualifying in any other Lodge as well as in this Lodge, providing a brother has a certificate to that effect, under seal of a Lodge in good standing ; *provided*, that any member of the Degree of Truth may be elected if all qualified brothers refuse to serve, and a dispensation be granted by the Grand Master of the District previous to the election.

Sec. 4. All officers shall be clear of all pecuniary charges on the books at the time of installation.

Sec. 5. Nominations for elective offices shall be made only on the two meetings immediately preceding that of a regular election, except when the nominees for an office all decline.

Sec. 6. Officers shall be elected by ballot at the first regular meeting in June and December of each year, and be installed at the first regular meeting in January and July of each year, *provided*, the installing officers be present; if absent, the Lodge may, by vote, defer it for one week, or call a special meeting for the purpose, at the request of the District Deputy Grand Master.

Sec. 7. Any officer absenting himself from the Lodge for three successive meetings, except in case of sickness, or any officer for misconduct or neglect as such, may be removed by a vote of two-thirds of the members voting at the next regular meeting after a resolution therefor has been offered in the Lodge at a regular meeting.

Sec. 8. Vacancies in any elective office may be filled by the Lodge by nomination and election, by ballot, at the next regular meeting after nominating, and, until so filled, the Noble Grand shall appoint a member to the office *pro tem*.

Sec. 9. The duties of the various officers shall be as laid down in the charges of office, and as specified by this Constitution, and the By-Laws of the Lodge.

SEC. 10. The Noble Grand, or officer acting as such, shall appoint the majority, and the Vice-Grand, or officer acting as such, the minority of all committees on candidates or charges.

SEC. 11. The Lodge, at any regular meeting within two months previous to the second Tuesday in May, of each year, shall elect 'one representative to the Grand Lodge for its members of fifty or under ; also one representative of every fifty members over and above said first number of fifty, and one for every fraction exceeding thirty members in good standing as shown by its report on the 31st day of December of the previous year ; the date of such election having been fixed by a vote of the Lodge at least one week prior thereto.

SEC. 12. No member holding an office relating to the management or disbursement of Lodge funds shall be eligible to any other office of similar character in the same Lodge during the term of office to which he was first elected.

SEC. 13. At all elections provided for by Sections 6 and 8 of this Article, if there be but one candidate for an office, such candidate may be elected by acclamation.

SEC. 14. No member who is more than thirteen weeks in arrears for weekly or funeral dues, shall be entitled to the term pass-word or to vote in the Lodge.

Sec. 15. No member shall be eligible for election as Treasurer or Trustee of a Lodge who is indebted to the Lodge for any borrowed money, or held as security to the Lodge for any indebtedness due the Lodge ; nor shall a Treasurer or Trustee be permitted to borrow or use any funds of the Lodge, or become surety for the same.

ARTICLE VII.

DUTIES OF OFFICERS.

Section 1. It shall be the duty of the Noble Grand to preside at all sessions of the Lodge, and enforce a due observance of the Constitution and By-Laws ; to see that all officers, members and committees of the Lodge perform their respective duties, as enjoined by the several charges and laws ; to appoint all officers and committees not otherwise provided for ; he shall not be entitled to vote, except at the election of officers and when balloting for candidates ; when the members are equally divided on other questions, he shall give the casting vote, excepting in cases of appeal from his decision ; he shall inspect and announce the result of all ballotings, or other votes by the Lodge ; sign all orders drawn by the Recording Secretary on the Treasury for moneys legally voted, and, previous to closing, require the Permanent Secretary to read the receipts of the evening, and ask the Treasurer if he has received the same. He shall, also, on the evening of installation, appoint a Finance Committee to serve for the term, consisting of three members not having charge of the Lodge funds.

SEC. 2. The Vice Grand shall assist the Noble Grand in the performance of his duties ; under his direction have charge of the door ; preside over the Lodge in the absence of the Noble Grand ; shall examine and ascertain the condition of the ballot when balloting for candidates for membership, and perform all other duties required by the charges and usages of the Order.

SEC. 3. The Recording Secretary shall keep accurate minutes of Lodge proceedings ; endorse and file all papers and documents pertaining to Lodge transactions ; issue, sign and attest, when required by the Lodge or the laws and usages of the Order, all cards, certificates, drafts and other official documents, and affix thereto the Lodge seal, which shall be in his charge and keeping ; number serially and file all communications from the Grand Master or Grand Secretary, and enter an abstract thereof, and the number, on the minutes ; make out (with the assistance of the Permanent Secretary, if any) the term and relief reports ; give without vote, to any qualified brother, a certificate of his standing in the Lodge to enable him to join an Encampment, or a Rebekah Degree Lodge ; give the notice required by Section 8 of Article VIII, of this Con-

stitution ; endorse on propositions for membership
the names of the Committee of Investigation, and
notify them of their appointment ; notify persons
elected to membership when to appear for initiation or admission ; keep a roll of the members,
with a record of the degrees and rank they have
attained, and perform such other duties as are or
may be required by the laws, charges and usages
of the Order. He may receive such compensation
for his services as the Lodge may determine.

SEC. 4. The Permanent Secretary (or Secretary,
should there be no Permanent Secretary) shall
keep just and true accounts between the Lodge and
its members, or others, in a regular set of books,
including ledger, journal, receipt and cash books,
and such others as may be required by the Lodge
and the laws and usages of the Order. He shall
also keep a book in which the residence of each
member is recorded, and in which he shall note
any change of the same. He shall receive and receipt for all money due the Lodge, and pay the
same to the Treasurer at each Lodge meeting. He
shall give the notices required by Section 1 of Article VIII of this Constitution, and shall keep a
copy of the same, or the substance thereof, with
the date, on a stub to be retained by him in a book
prepared for that purpose ; endorse cards of visi-
tors ; during the months of June and December of
each year, and previous to the last meeting in said

months, notify each member who is in any way indebted to the Lodge, of the state of his account; assist the Recording Secretary in making his term reports, and render to the Lodge, at the close of each term, an abstract of all accounts on the Lodge books, together with the receipts and expenditures of the term. He shall also furnish at each election a list of the members entitled to vote, to the Noble Grand; under his direction call the same, and perform such other duties as may be required by the Lodge, and the laws and usages of the Order. The Permanent Secretary may receive such compensation for his services as the Lodge may determine.

SEC. 5. The Treasurer, prior to installation, shall give a joint and several bond, payable to the Trustees, in trust for the Lodge, in the sum of not less than one thousand dollars, with two or more sureties, for the faithful performance of his duty; receive from the Permanent Secretary, each Lodge night, the money in his hands; pay all orders drawn on him by the Noble Grand by authority of the Lodge, and attested by the Recording Secretary under the seal thereof; give when requested by the Noble Grand a statement, in writing, of money on hand; report at the first meeting of each month, the receipts and expenditures of the preceding month, with balance on hand; at the last meeting of each term report the term receipts and expenditures, and exhibit vouchers; and have his books written up for examination by the Finance Committee within twenty-four hours thereafter.

SEC; 6. The Trustees (if there be any) shall give a joint and several bond in such sum as may be required, for the faithful performance of their duties, to be approved by the Lodge, and made payable to the Noble Grand and Vice Grand, with two good and sufficient sureties for each Trustee, *provided*, that each Trusteee may execute a sepa rate bond with two sureties as aforesaid, if he so elect. The Board of Trustees shall hold in trust all stocks, sureties, investments, property and funds belonging to this Lodge, and transfer, exchange or deposit the same, or any part thereof, when required by the Lodge so to do; and shall also keep the funds invested for the best interests of the Lodge, in such stocks, bonds or other securities, as shall be approved of by a two-thirds vote of the members present at a regular meeting, or deposit the same in some savings bank. It shall be their duty to have the general supervision of the widows and orphans of deceased members of the Lodge, and render them such assistance as the Lodge may direct, or the rules and usages of the Order may require. On the expiration of their term of office, or removal therefrom, they shall deliver to their successors in office, or such persons as shall be appointed, all the books, papers, bonds or other property they may have in their hands belonging to the Lodge. They shall keep a full and correct account of all money received, expended or invested, and at the close of each semi-annual term, make a full report in writing of all business transacted by them during the term, together with a particular statement of the funds and investments belonging to the Lodge.

SEC. 7. The Warden shall canvass all votes, when directed by the Noble Grand, and perform the other duties of his office.

SEC. 8. The Outside Guardian, in addition to the duties of his office, shall, under the Warden, take care of the regalia and Lodge room, and may receive such compensation for his services as the Lodge may determine.

SEC. 9. The Noble Grand may appoint a Chaplain, who shall open and close regular meetings with prayer and perform such other appropriate duties as the Lodge may direct.

SEC. 10. The Acting Past Grand shall attend all regular meetings, deliver the charge of his office, and act as Outside Conductor when required by the Noble Grand.

SEC. 11. All other officers shall perform such duties as are prescribed for them by the regulations of the Order, this Constitution or the By-Laws of this Lodge.

SEC. 12. Any Lodge may provide in its By-Laws for the acceptance of the guarantee of an incorporated security company in place of the bonds provided for in this Article, for the faithful performance of their respective duties by the financial officers of the Lodge.

ARTICLE VIII.

PENALTIES AND TRIALS.

SECTION I.—*Clause* 1, Any member neglecting or refusing to make payment of his dues or demands against him to the Lodge, according to its By-Laws, for the space of eleven months, shall be notified by the Lodge, which notice shall be sent to his last given address, of the state of his account ; if his account still remains unsettled, the fact of his dues and demands against him being so in arrears and unpaid shall be announced in open Lodge at the last two regular meetings previous to the time he would be twelve months in arrears, and if his account still remains unsettled, he shall, when he is twelve months in arrears, be suspended from membership and so declared by the Noble Grand, unless otherwise determined by vote of the Lodge ; *provided*, that no person shall be suspended under this section while charges are pending against him, and provided that a member may, prior to suspension, pay a sufficient portion of the amount due to avoid suspension.

Clause 2. Any member suspended from membership for non-payment of dues may be reinstated in the Lodge from which he was suspended within one year thereafter, by paying the amount of one year's dues and by receiving a vote of two-thirds of the members present—a motion to that effect having been laid over one week ; but *after* one year, he may be reinstated upon the payment of the fee charged for an initiate of the same age, as provided by the By-Laws, or such lesser sum as may be fixed by the By-Laws of the Lodge to which such application is made ; *provided*, such sum be not less than the amount of one year's dues of said Lodge ; and he shall petition the Lodge, in writing, to be reinstated, which shall be disposed of, in all respects, as provided for in Article III, Section 1, for petitions for membership by initiation.

Clause 3. A member suspended from membership for non-payment of dues, and who makes application for reinstatement and for a withdrawal card for the purpose of uniting with another Lodge in this jurisdiction, may be reinstated and granted a final card at any time within five years from the date of suspension, upon the payment of one year's dues and the usual price of a card.

· *Clause* 4. A member, after being suspended in this jurisdiction for non-payment of dues for the space of five years, wishing to join a Lodge in this jurisdiction, shall be entitled to receive, and the Lodge shall grant him, upon proper application, a dismissal certificate, upon the receipt of one dollar.

Clause 5. A member suspended from membership in this jurisdiction for non-payment of dues, wishing to regain membership in another jurisdiction, shall, upon proper application, be entitled to receive from the Lodge from which he was so suspended a dismissal certificate, upon the payment to said Lodge of one dollar.

Clause 6. In all cases, when a member has been suspended for non-payment of dues, and his Lodge has refused to reinstate him, he shall, upon proper application, be entitled to receive, and the Lodge shall grant a dismissal certificate, upon the receipt therefor of one dollar.

Clause 7. Dismissal certificates may be received from the holders thereof, on application for membership in Subordinate Lodges, in the same manner and with the same effect as withdrawal cards ; and applications made on such certificates shall be received and acted on in like manner as upon withdrawal cards. But the holders of such certificates shall in no case be allowed to visit thereon.

Clause 8. The certificates named in this section shall be only those provided by the Grand Secretary of the Sovereign Grand Lodge.

SEC. 2. Any member who shall violate any of the principles of the Order, or offend against the Constitution, By-Laws or Rules of Order of this Lodge, or the penal laws of the land, shall be fined, reprimanded, suspended or expelled, as the By-Laws may direct or the Lodge determine.

SEC. 3. Every member shall be entitled to a fair trial for any offense involving reprimand, suspension or expulsion. No member shall be put upon trial unless charges duly specifying the offense, so as fully to apprise him of the nature thereof, and to enable him to prepare for his defense, shall be submitted to the Lodge, in writing, and signed by a member of a Lodge within this jurisdiction, and a copy thereof, under seal of the Lodge, be served upon him.

SEC 4. Such charges shall be referred to a committee of five members, who shall, without unnecessary delay, summon the parties and try the case. They shall keep full minutes of the evidence and of their proceedings, and report the same to the Lodge, with their verdict. If a witness be a member of the Order, he shall give his evidence on the honor of an Odd Fellow; if he be not a member, then on oath or affirmation, and the proceedings must state that such obligation or oath was administered. No testimony shall be taken without notice or opportunity for cross examination by the opposing party. Upon the report being made, notice thereof shall forthwith be given, by the Secretary, to the party against whom the verdict is rendered, and he shall have two weeks in which to file his exceptions. If no exceptions are filed within two weeks, the Lodge shall proceed to pronounce judgment upon the verdict, and affix the penalty. An appeal from the judgment of the Lodge may be taken at any time within two weeks thereafter, to the Grand Lodge ; and if no such appeal is taken, the judgment of the Lodge shall be final. When a bill of exceptions to the report of the committee is filed, as above provided, the Lodge may determine upon its merits, and either sustain the report of the committee, or refer the same back to the same or another committee, or grant a new trial. If the Lodge deems the exceptions not well taken, it shall proceed to pronounce its judgment and affix the penalty.

SEC. 5. If the accused refuse or neglect to stand trial when duly summoned, the committee shall report him guilty of contempt of the Lodge, which report shall be conclusive, and the punishment shall be expulsion.

SEC. 6. If a specific penalty for an offense be provided in the Constitution or By-Laws, the Noble Grand shall enforce it. If none be so provided, the Lodge shall decide by paper ballot whether the penalty shall be expulsion, suspension or reprimand and fine. During the ballot, the accused brother shall withdraw from the Lodge room. If upon the first ballot it shall appear that two-thirds of the ballots are cast for expulsion, such shall be the penalty. If two-thirds of the ballots are not cast for expulsion, then the Lodge shall proceed to ballot for suspension ; and if two-thirds of the ballots are cast for suspension. suspension shall be the penalty, and the Lodge shall proceed to fix the duration of such suspension, which shall not exceed two years. If neither expulsion or suspension is determined as the penalty, as above provided, then the penalty shall either be reprimand, fine, or both ; if fine is determined upon, then the Lodge shall fix the amount, not exceeding ten dollars ; if reprimand is decided upon, then the accused shall be reprimanded in open Lodge by the acting Noble Grand. No ballot held under this section shall be reconsidered. All fines imposed under this section shall be charged to his account, and considered in determining his standing in the Lodge, as dues, and when the fine thus imposed, added to his dues, brings him under the penalty of Section 1 of this Article, he shall be notified, and allowed the usual time to make payment ; and if he ceases to be a member, he shall, prior to reinstatement, pay the whole amount of such fines and dues.

SEC. 7. When a member shall be subject to the penalty of reprimand, he shall be summoned to attend at some regular meeting. to be fixed by the Noble Grand, to be reprimanded from the chair of the Noble Grand ; and until he so attend and be reprimanded he shall be suspended from all benefits and privileges of membership.

SEC. 8. Notice of all suspensions, expulsions, rejections and reinstatements, and of brothers who

have been suspended in accordance with Section 1
of this Article, shall forthwith be forwarded to
every Lodge in the county; to the Subordinate
Encampment and Rebekah Degree Lodge of which
the brother is a member, and to the Grand Secretary.

SEC. 9. An expelled member can be reinstated
only after a proposition, reference and election by
ballot, as in the case of a newly proposed member,
permission having first been obtained from the
Grand Master A brother suspended for any cause
may be reinstated on the removal of the cause or
the expiration of the term for which he was suspended, without action of the Lodge, and the
Noble Grand shall declare in open Lodge his being
reinstated.

SEC. 10. Any member intending to appeal from
the action of the Lodge, either on a decision of law,
or where charges have been preferred, shall file with
the Secretary a notice of his appeal and the grounds
thereof; upon which the Secretary shall forthwith
send a certified copy of the same, together with a
certified copy of all charges, reports, evidence and
proceedings of the Lodge relating to the case, to
the Grand Secretary, to be presented to the Committee on Appeals of the Grand Lodge. In cases
involving the good standing of the member with
his Lodge, if such member shall die before the
time for filing his notice of appeal has expired, any

person pecuniarily interested in the result of the
case as beneficiary, heir or legal representative of
such deceased member, may be substituted in
place of such deceased member and thereafter prosecute said case to final determination.

SEC. 11. An appeal by any member from the
action of the Lodge authorizing the payment of
money from the funds thereof, shall stop the payment of such money by the Lodge until the appeal has been heard and decided by the proper authority. A notice of appeal by a member, duly
filed with the Secretary, in writing, shall also stop
the payment of money as aforesaid, for the period
of two weeks, after which time, if no appeal be
perfected by any member, the money shall be
paid.

ARTICLE IX.

FUNDS AND PROPERTY.

SECTION 1. The funds and property of this
Lodge shall be held exclusively as a Trust Fund to
be devoted to no other purpose than the charitable
uses of the I. O. O. F., and expenditures legiti-
mately made for Lodge purposes, and the advance-
ment of the interests of the Lodge or Order. The
funds may be invested from time to time as the
Lodge shall direct, but no part thereof or of the
Lodge property, or of the proceeds of any sales of
such property, shall ever be divided among the

members; and in case of a surrender or forfeiture of the Lodge charter, all the funds and property of the Lodge, of whatsoever kind, shall be immediately surrendered and delivered up to the Grand Lodge of this jurisdiction, or to its officers or agents properly authorized to receive them.

ARTICLE X.

OFFENSES.

SECTION 1. No member of this Lodge shall be concerned in organizing or visiting any illegal, spurious, expelled, extinct or suspended Lodge of Odd Fellows. No member shall receive or put any motion from the chair of the Noble Grand, unless he be a present or past Noble Grand or Vice Grand, except that the Right Supporter to the Noble Grand, when occupying the chair of the Noble Grand temporarily, may entertain a motion, put the question and declare the result.

SEC. 2. This Lodge shall not have a public procession unless to attend the funeral of a member, nor have any public celebration of any kind, nor get up any ball or public amusement in the name of the Order, nor admit to membership any member of an expelled or extinct Lodge, nor reninstate an expelled or suspended member of this Lodge, without permission of the Grand Master, *provided*, that District Deputy Grand Masters are authorized to grant dispensations to hold public processions,

balls or amusements of a similar character, in the
name of the Order and where the regalia of the
Order may be worn, in accordance with Article IV,
Section 7, of the Constitution of the Grand Lodge.

SEC. 3. No member of this Lodge shall exhibit
or in any way use, for business purposes, or upon
his business card or sign, any emblem of the Order,
nor any name by which this Order or any of its
branches are known ; and no member of this Lodge
shall become or continue a member or officer of
any association or corporation using such emblem
or name for business purposes. Any member vio-
lating any of the provisions of this section shall,
upon conviction thereof, be suspended for not less
than one year, or expelled, as the Lodge may determine. The provisions of this section shall not
apply to Odd Fellows' Library, Hall, Cemetery or
Mutual Aid Associations, nor to corporations or
associations now existing which are *bona fide* in
process of dissolution, and which shall in good
faith prosecute such dissolution to completion
within a reasonable time.

ARTICLE XI.

TERMS AND RETURNS.

SECTION I. All terms shall commence on the
first day of January and July in each year, and end
on the day on which the succeeding one com-
mences.

SEC. 2. The officers for the term about expiring shall prepare and deliver to the officers who shall install their successors, the result of the elections, and a report of the work of the term, including the names of those admitted, whether by Initiation, by Card, as an Ancient Odd Fellow or by Dismissal Certificate, together with their age, nativity, occupation and rank; also, those suspended and expelled, and the cause thereof, those reinstated and deceased, the number of degrees conferred, the whole number in membership, and amount of receipts, accompanied by whatever amount may be due to the Grand Lodge.

SEC. 3. In addition to the above, the officers for the term expiring on the first meeting in January, shall annually make to the Grand Lodge a full return of the members of the Lodge, ranked according to the degrees attained, and a statement of the number of members relieved in the past year; the number of widowed families relieved; the number of members buried; the number of sisters buried; the amount of money applied for each of these purposes; the amount paid for the education of orphans; the amount of money in the Treasury, the amount of Widows' and Orphans' Fund, the amount and nature of investments, the amount paid for charity, and the amount paid for current expenses.

SEC. 4. Should this Lodge fail to make any of its returns, as required by the two preceding sections, for one year, it shall thereby forfeit its charter and become extinct ; and it shall be the duty of the Grand Master or District Deputy Grand Master to withhold the Annual Traveling Password and Semi-annual Password until such returns are made and the amount due the Grand Lodge paid. And it shall be the duty of the last installed officers to transmit or surrender to the Grand Master or his Deputy, the Charter, books, papers, furniture and funds of the Lodge.

ARTICLE XII.

CARDS.

SECTION 1. Withdrawal Cards may be granted to members who are clear of the books, according to law, by a majority vote, by ballot, of the members present when application is made. Should the Lodge refuse to grant the card, the applicant, on tendering a written resignation of membership, and paying all dues, shall be entitled to receive from the Secretary a certificate, under seal of the Lodge, to that effect ; and such certificate shall be sufficient evidence of good standing at the time of such resignation.

SEC. 2. Visiting Cards may be granted upon application in open Lodge, or they may be issued by the Noble Grand and Recording Secretary to members in good standing upon application in writing, but in either case the dues of the applicant must be paid up to the end of the time for which the card is granted, which time shall not exceed one year from the date of the card.

ARTICLE XIII.
INTERPRETATION—AMENDMENT.

SECTION 1. When any doubt arises as to the true meaning of any part of these Articles, it shall be determined by the Grand Lodge.

SEC. 2. These Articles, or any part thereof, shall not be altered, amended or annulled, except on motion made in the Grand Lodge, at a regular session.

ARTICLE XIV.
BY-LAWS.

SECTION 1. This Lodge may make, alter or rescind such By-Laws, Rules and Resolutions, from time to time, as may be deemed expedient, *provided*, that they do not in any wise contravene this Constitution or the Constitution, By-Laws or Regulations of the Grand Lodge of the State of California, or of the Sovereign Grand Lodge, I. O. O. F.

SEC. 2. The By-Laws of this Lodge shall be in force from the time the Lodge shall have received notice of their approval by the Committee on Laws of Subordinates, subject to the approval of the Grand Lodge; and the manuscript copy of such By-Laws shall immediately after their adoption by the Lodge, and before being printed, be transmitted to the Grand Secretary, to be submitted to the Committee on Laws of Subordinates for their approval.

W. B. LYON, *Grand Secretary.*

BY-LAWS

—OF—

Petaluma Lodge, No. 30,

I. O. O. F.

——➤◇◄——

ARTICLE I.

MEETINGS.

SECTION 1. The regular meetings of this Lodge shall be held on Tuesday evening of each week. The hour of meeting shall be at eight o'clock during the months of June, July and August; at seven o'clock during the months of December, January and February; and at half-past seven o'clock during the remaining months of the year. The Lodge shall be opened within fifteen minutes after the appointed time; and in the absence of the Noble Grand and Vice Grand, a Past Grand shall take the chair.

SEC. 2. Special meetings may be called by the Noble Grand, at discretion, or on the written request of five members, or by vote of the Lodge; and the Recording Secretary shall put notice thereof in a newspaper of this city, or on the bulletin board. No business shall be done except that specified in the call.

SEC. 3. At all meetings, five members, including one qualified to preside, shall be a quorum.

SEC 4. If, fifteen minutes after the time for opening, no member qualified to take the chair be present, the Recording Secretary shall call the brothers to order, enter in his minutes the facts, and adjourn. If the Secretary be absent, the brothers may select a Chairman, appoint a Secretary, who shall make a memorandum of the facts, and then adjourn ; and such memorandum shall be entered on the minutes of the next regular meeting.

ARTICLE II.

MEMBERSHIP AND DUES.

SECTION 1. Applications for membership must be accompanied with the fee fixed by the By-Laws. No candidate shall be initiated on the night of his election, except on a two-thirds vote. Every person admitted to membership shall sign the Constitution and By-Laws, and his membership dates from that time.

SEC 2. Persons admitted to membership shall pay the following fees, to wit:

By Initiation or by Dismissal Certificate.

If 25 years old, or under.................... ....$10 00
From 25 to 40, each additional year 50
From 40 to 50, each additional year. 1 00
Over 50, each additional year 3 00

By Deposit of Card in Date.

If 25 years old, or under.................................... $ 5 co
From 25 to 40, each additional year............... .. 50
From 40 to 50, each additional year.................. 1 co
Over 50, each additional year................ .... 3 oo

As Ancient Odd Fellows.

If 25 years old, or under................. ....$10 00
From 25 to 40, each additional year................ 50
From 40 to 50, each additional year....•............ 1 00
Over 50, each additional year............ .... 3 co

By Reinstatement.

If reinstated after suspension for non-payment of
dues, he shall pay the fee fixed by Section I,
Article VIII, of the Constitution.

If reinstated after expulsion, he shall pay $25.

SEC. 3. Each member shall pay, as dues, the
sum of one dollar per month, in advance.

SEC. 4 If the money and funds of the Lodge be
exhausted, the Lodge may levy an equal assess-
ment on each member for the relief of sick or dis-
tressed members, or to pay necessary Lodge expenses.

ARTICLE III.

FUNDS.

Benefits, relief or current expenses may be paid
at a regular meeting by vote of a majority of the
members present and entitled to vote ; but Lodge

money, funds or property shall not be disposed of except a resolution offered at a regular meeting, and laid over at least one week, and then be adopted by a two-thirds vote; *provided*, that no loan of the Lodge funds shall be made to members.

ARTICLE IV.

BENEFITS.

SECTION 1. Each member, not disqualified, in case of sickness or accident rendering him incapable of earning a living, shall be paid by the Lodge the following sums per week during such sickness or disability, commencing not more than one week prior to being reported sick to the Lodge, provided he was able to have such report made, unless he be over ten miles from this city (but a fraction of a week shall not be counted): Initiates, $2.00; members of the First Degree, $4.00; members of the Second Degree, $6.00; members of the Third Degree, $8.00; *provided,* ~~that benefits shall not be paid for the first week's sickness, and provided further,~~ that when any member has received from this Lodge, as sick benefits; the sum of $600, then thereafter he shall receive, if an initiate, $1.00; member of the First Degree, $2.00; member of the Second Degree, $3.00; member of the Third Degree, $4.00; *provided,* such sickness or disability be not caused by intemperance or immoral conduct or constitutional disease or bodily infirmity existing at his admission, and intentionally concealed from the Lodge.

SEC. 2. A brother taken sick not over ten miles from this city, shall cause himself to be so reported to the Noble Grand, Vice Grand or to the Lodge.

SEC. 3. A brother taken sick over ten miles from this city, claiming benefits, shall send to the Noble Grand or the Lodge, a true statement of his case, attested by the Noble Grand of the Lodge of Odd Fellows nearest to him, under its seal ; or if no Lodge be within five miles of him, the same be stated by the certificate of a respectable physician, a magistrate, a master of a vessel or an American Consul. And such statement shall be sent every four weeks, if the sickness continue.

SEC. 4. If, from the nature of the sickness or disability, or for any reason it be impossible, or impracticable for the brother to comply with Sections 2 and 3, next preceding, he shall nevertheless, be entitled to benefits. Provided, a member though sick or partially disabled, and who having such work to do, can go out to collect debts, make contracts, settle accounts, or superintend his his business, shall not be entitled to benefits as a legal right, but may be granted benefits by a three-fourths vote of the the members present and entitled to vote.

SEC. 5. On the death of a brother fifty dollars shall be paid towards his funeral expenses ; and on the death of the wife of a brother, *in good standing*, twenty-five dollars shall be paid. If no funeral expenses are incurred by the Order, or the dependent relatives by the death of a brother or his wife, no appropriation shall be made from the funds of the Lodge.

ARTICLE V.

FUNERALS.

SECTION I. On the death of a brother within the jurisdiction of this Lodge, the Noble Grand, aided by the other officers, shall prepare for the funeral (unless otherwise requested by the nearest relatives of deceased), and summon members to attend by notice duly given. The bulletin board at the main entrance to the Lodge room shall be placed in public view, on which the Secretary shall give notice of the funeral of the brother, with time and place thereof, and hoist the flag on the hall at half-mast, immediately after the Noble Grand has instructed him so to do, which shall be considered a due notice to members of the Lodge.

SEC. 2. Members shall be required to attend all funerals when duly notified thereof.

ARTICLE VI.

FINES AND PENALTIES.

SECTION I. No member who is more than thirteen weeks in arrears for dues, assessments or fines shall be entitled to receive benefits in case of sickness, nor be entitled to receive benefits by reason of any payments he may make during such sickness or disability.

SEC. 2. A member of the Visiting Committee neglecting his duty, shall be fined not less than five dollars, or suspended or expelled.

SEC. 3. A member of any other committee neglecting his duty, shall be fined two dollars.

SEC. 4. Each elective officer absent when the Lodge is opened, shall be fined one dollar, and each appointed officer shall be fined fifty cents. The fine to be entered at the first meeting when the officer is present and not excused.

SEC. 5. Such absentees shall render in open Lodge one of the following excuses, to wit: absence from the city, sickness of self or family, attendance on the sick or dead, or at a funeral, or on Lodge or public duty.

SEC. 6 An officer or member who may have been fined, may appeal to the Lodge to have his fine remitted, and if the appeal be sustained by a vote of two-thirds of all the members present, the fine shall be remitted.

ARTICLE VII.

DEGREES.

No degrees shall be granted to a member in arrears for dues, or against whom there are fines or

assessments unpaid, or charges undecided. Five
dollars shall be charged for each degree.

ARTICLE VIII.

CARDS AND DISMISSAL CERTIFICATES.

SECTION 1. Visiting and Withdrawal Cards may
be granted to members clear of the books, as per
Article XII of the Constitution, by payment of
fifty cents for the former, and one dollar for the
latter.

SEC. 2. Dismissal certificates are issued by the
Noble Grand and Recording Secretary, without
vote, after application in open Lodge under
clauses 4, 5, 6, Section 1, Article VIII, of the Constitution.

ARTICLE IX.

BALLOTS AND ELECTIONS.

SECTION 1. When ballots are taken, the ballot-
box shall be placed on a pedestal, in front and in
full view of the Noble Grand. Members shall advance singly, and deposit their ballots, which shall
be inspected by the Noble Grand and Vice Grand,
and the result declared to the Lodge by the N. G.

SEC. 2. At elections for officers, the Warden
(with two tellers appointed by the Noble Grand)
shall receive the votes in the ballot-box, and canvass them, counting blank ballots, or ballots for a
person not nominated, as votes, and declare the re-

sult to the Noble Grand, who shall announce it to
the Lodge. A majority of the ballots cast shall be
necessary to elect. If on the second ballot there
be no choice, a third ballot shall be taken between
the two brothers having the most votes on the second ballot.

ARTICLE X.

OFFICERS AND THEIR DUTIES.

VICE GRAND.

SEC. 1. The vice Grand shall, under the direction of the Noble Grand, have special charge of the
door.

TRUSTEES.

SEC. 2. Three Trustees shall be elected by ballot at the regular election in December of each
year.

SEC 3. They shall transact all their business
when met together as a Board, and the consent of
a majority shall be necessary to each act. They
shall keep a book in which shall be entered all
their transactions as Trustees, so that every kind
of Lodge property in their hands shall distinctly
appear therein, and perform such other duties as
are required of them by the Constitution.

ARTICLE XI.

FINANCE COMMITTEE.

SECTION 1. The Finance Committee shall examine all claims and accounts against the Lodge,

of whatsoever kind, when referred to them, and report thereon in writing, over their own signatures, as soon as practicable. They shall inspect the books, and audit the accounts of the Permanent Secretary, Treasurer and Trustees of the Lodge, and report thereon in writing at the first regular meeting in each term, or whenever required by the Lodge.

VISITING COMMITTEE.

SEC. 2. The Visiting Committee shall consist of the Noble Grand, Vice Grand, Warden, Conductor, Right Supporter to Noble Grand, Left Supporter to Noble Grand, and Right Supporter to Vice Grand. Each member thereof shall visit each sick brother as follows: Wednesday, Left Supporter to Noble Grand ; Thursday, Right Supporter to Vice Grand ; Friday, Warden ; Saturday, Vice Grand ; Sunday, Conductor ; Monday, Right Supporter to Noble Grand ; Tuesday, Noble Grand. The Noble Grand shall visit each brother reported sick with'n twenty-four hours thereafter, if within the city limits, and within forty-eight hours if outside the city limits, and not over ten miles distant *pro] vided*, that in the latter case he deem such visit necessary), and see that brothers are cared for, according to law, during their sickness. If it becomes necessary, he may employ a nurse to attend upon a sick member, at the expense of the Lodge, and report, at each regular meeting of the

Lodge, the number of nurses employed, and the amount so charged against the Lodge.

ARTICLE XII.

RESIDENCE OF MEMBERS.

SECTION 1. Each member, when he signs the Constitution and By-Laws, shall give his exact residence to the Permanent Secretary, who shall enter it in a book kept for that purpose; and in case of removal, he shall notify the Secretary thereof within thirty days.

SEC. 2. A notice to a member by the proper Secretary shall be a legal notice, if sent through the Postoffice of this city addressed to him, at his residence, as per such book; except where personal or other notice is herein provided for.

ARTICLE XIII,

REPORTS OF COMMITTEES.

SECTION 1. Reports of committees and officers, except Visiting Committees, shall be in writing, and signed by a majority thereof.

ARTICLE XIV.

EXPLANATION OF WORDS.

SECTION 1. Whenever the word "Member" or "Members," "Brother" or "Brothers," is used in these By-Laws, it means Member or Brother of this Lodge.

SEC. 2. The phrase "two-thirds vote" means two-thirds of those present and entitled to vote.

ARTICLE XV.

AMENDMENTS, ETC.

SECTION 1. No part of these By-Laws shall be amended or repealed, except by resolution offered at a regular meeting, laid over at least one week, and adopted by a two-thirds vote.

SEC. 2. All former By-Laws and Rules are hereby repealed.

———

L. ELLSWORTH,
E. E. DREES,
W. F. FARRELL.
Committee on By-Laws.

———

Approved August 21, 189c.

CHARLES C. TERRILL,
GEORGE T. SHAW,
A. J. CLEARY,
Committee on Laws of Subordinates.

ORDER OF BUSINESS.

———

1. Opening.
2. Introduction of Visiting Brothers.
3. Calling the Roll of Officers.
4. Reading Minutes of last Meeting.
5. Report of Visiting Committee. Brothers Sick to be reported.
6. Ordering Drafts for Benefits.
7. Reports of Committees of Investigation.
8. Candidates Admitted.
9. Propositions for Membership.
10. Bills Presented.
11. Reports of Finance Committee.
12. Reports of Special Committees.
13. Unfinished Business on the Minutes.
14. Absentees of Previous Meetings Called.
15 Communications Read.
16. Applications for Cards.
17. Applications for and Conferring Degrees.
18. Other New Business.
19. Good of the Order.
20. Permanent Secretary's Report.
21. Closing.

RULES OF ORDER.

OPENING.

RULE 1. When the N. G. takes the chair, the officers and brothers shall take their respective stations, clothed in appropriate regalia, and at the sound of the gavel there shall be general silence, and after examining the brothers in the Lodge, if there be a Chaplain, then join with him in prayer. The Lodge shall then open in due form.

APPEALS.

RULE 2. The N. G. shall preserve order, and to that end may impose a fine of not less than $2 nor more than $10, subject to appeal to the Lodge ; announce the decisions of the Lodge on all subjects. He shall decide questions of order without debate (unless, entertaining doubts on the point, he invite it), subject to an appeal to the Lodge by any brother, on which appeal no brother shall speak more than once, when the question before the Lodge shall be: "Shall the decision of the Noble Grand stand as the judgment of the Lodge?"

MOTIONS.

RULE 3. No question shall be stated unless moved and seconded, nor be open for consideration until stated by the N. G., ; and when a question is before the Lodge no motion shall be received, un-

less first, to lie on the table ; second, the previous
question ; third, to postpone to a particular time ;
fourth, to postpone indefinitely ; fifth, to recom-
mit ; sixth, to refer ; seventh, to amend ; and they
shall have precedence in the order in which they
are here arranged, and the first two shall be decided without debate.

RULE 4. No motion shall be made by one
brother while another is speaking, and no motion
shall be made or seconded without rising and addressing the N. G.

RULE 5. Any brother making a motion shall
reduce the same to writing at the request of the
N. G, or any brother, in which case it shall not be
entertained until so written, and read from the
Secretary's desk.

RULE 6. No resolution shall be offered to the
Lodge except in writing, and signed by the member offering the same.

CALLED TO ORDER.

RULE 7. No brother shall be interrupted while
speaking, except it be to call him to order, or for
the purpose of explanation.

RULE 8. If a brother while speaking be called
to order, he shall, at the request of the N. G., take
his seat until the question of order is determined ;
when, if permitted, he may again proceed.

RULE 9. When a brother has been called to order for the manifestation of temper or improper

feeling, he shall not be allowed to speak again at that meeting, unless by special permission of the Lodge.

WHO MAY SPEAK, AND WHEN.

RULE 10. No brother shall speak without rising in his place, respectfully addressing the N. G. by his title, and having his name announced by the N. G. Brothers shall confine themselves to the question under debate, and avoid all personalities and indecorous or sarcastic language.

RULE 11. If two or more brothers rise to speak at the same time, the N. G. shall decide which is entitled to the floor. And no brother shall speak more than once, on the same subject or question, until all who wish to speak have had an opportunity to do so; nor more than twice without permission of the N. G. Each brother, while speaking, shall designate the brother spoken of by his proper rank or title, according to his standing in the Order.

BLANKS.

RULE 12. When a blank is to be filled, the question shall be first taken on the highest sum or number, and the longest time proposed.

TO DIVIDE A QUESTION.

RULE 13. Any brother may call for a division of a question, when the sense will admit of it; and on any five of the brothers calling for the ayes and noes, they shall be ordered by the N. G., and recorded in the minutes.

RULE 14. The Noble Grand or any member doubting the decision of a question may call for a division of the Lodge, which shall be by rising and standing until counted; but a division cannot be called for after the Noble Grand has announced the result of the vote.

PUTTING THE QUESTION.

RULE 15. Before putting the question, the N. G. shall ask: "Is the Lodge ready for the question?" If no brother rises to speak, the N. G. shall rise and put it, and after he has risen to put the question, no brother shall be permitted to speak upon it. While the N. G. is addressing the Lodge or putting the question, silence shall be observed.

TO RECONSIDER.

RULE 16. After any question except one of indefinite postponement has been decided, any two brothers who voted in the majority, may, at the same or next regular meeting, move for a reconsideration thereof; but no discussion of the main question shall be allowed unless reconsidered.

VOTING.

RULE 17. No member shall vote on any question in which he is immediately interested.

SEC. 18. Every member present (not in arrears) shall vote, if in proper regalia, unless for special reasons ; *provided*, this rule does not interfere with the provisions of the By-Laws regarding new members, etc.

POINTS OF ORDER.

RULE 19. In speaking on points of order, the N. G. shall have precedence, but he cannot speak on any other subject, except to state facts within his own knowledge, without previously vacating his chair, and filling it with a qualified officer or brother.

RETIRING.

RULE 20. No brother shall retire without leave of the N. G., and during opening. initiation, recess, reading of the minutes, taking the ayes and noes, roll-call, or closing, the doors shall be kept closed.

PREVIOUS QUESTION.

RULE 21. On the call of three brothers for the previous question, the N. G. shall put the question in this form ; "Shall the main question be now put ?" If the motion is carried, the vote shall first be upon all pending amendments, after which upon the main question. If decided in the negative, the question shall lie over until the next regular meeting.

COMMITTEES.

RULE 22. The first brother named on a committee shall act as Chairman until another is chosen by the members of the committee. (The mover of a resolution referred to a special committee is usually the first named thereon.)

RULE 23. Any brother may excuse himself from serving on a committee, if, at the time of his appointment he is a member of two other committees. No member can be appointed on a committee when absent from the Lodge.

RULE 24. No committee can be finally discharged until all the debts contracted by it shall have been paid.

TO ADJOURN.

RULE 25. A motion to close is always in order after the regular business is concluded (provided no brother has the floor), which motion shall be decided without debate. If decided in the affirmative, the Lodge shall then be closed in due form.

RULE 26. Cushing's Manual shall govern all cases not provided for in these Rules.

RULE. 27. These Rules of Order may be altered or amended after one week's notice in writing being given at a regular meeting, specifying the proposed alteration or amendment ; but any one of them, or any clause thereof, may be suspended for the time being by a vote of two thirds of all qualified members present.

PRAYERS.

OPENING PRAYER.

Almighty and most merciful God! we adore Thee as the Creator of all worlds, and the righteous Governor of all beings, upon whom we are all dependent for life and all its blessings, and without whose favor no human enterprise can permanently prosper. Lift upon us, we pray Thee, O Lord, the light of Thy countenance, and bless us while we are together this evening. May all things be done in the spirit of charity and brotherly kindness, and our labors of love be blessed to the promotion of the best interests of our beloved Order. Hear us, O God, in behalf of the stranger, the sick, the afflicted, the widow and the orphan, and bless them as Thou seest they may need. Keep us ever in Thy fear and wisdom, and save us all with an everlasting salvation; and to Thy great name be all the glory, as it was in the beginning, is now, and ever shall be, world without end. Amen.

CLOSING PRAYER.

We bless Thee, O Lord, that we have been permitted to enjoy this, another Lodge meeting. Pardon what Thou hast seen amiss in us; and now, as we are about to depart and separate, let Thy blessing be with us, and with all our brethren throughout the Globe. May brotherly love prevail, and every moral and social virtue adorn our lives, while members of this Lodge below; and at last may we be admitted to the joys of a better world; and to Thee shall be all the praise and glory, for ever and ever. Amen.

CHARTER MEMBERS.

Daniel McLaren
Stephen C. Hayden
Silas M. Martin
Thomas McMurray

E. S. McMurray
Stephen Payran
Charles Purvine
William Ayres

PAST GRANDS.

Atwater, Henry Heaton
Anderson, F. A
Batman, James W.
Brown, William S.
Bauer, J. Wm.
Crawford, Isaac S
Campbell, Joseph
Cowen, Joseph A.
Corliss, William B.
Drees, E. E.
Doyle, Frank P.
Dryden, C. C.
Edelman, G. W.
Elder, James W.
Ellsworth, Lee
Ellsworth, Henry L.
Fernald, Johnson
Fritsch, John
Fritsch, Walter S.
Farrell, William F.
Fulmer, J. B.
Harris, J. W.
Haskell, William B.
Harris, William S.
Hopkins, Samuel J.
Hopes, Edward
Jenks, George H.

Johnson, J. E.
Knowles, James H.
Kill, James M.
Martin, Silas M.
Meyer, J. F
Newburgh, E.
Nay, L. G
Oster, Henry
Pinim, Henry
Putnam, D. W. C.
Poehlmann, Conrad
Rowlson, E.
Ross, David
Sackett, D. A.
Sloper, W.
Spotswood, George W.
Spotswood, Robert H.
Sproule, J.
St. John, S. C.
Toms, Samuel A.
Wiswell, J. A.
Weber, Martin
Ward, A.
Weber, William N.
Young, C. M.
Zartman, William
Zartman, William H.

ALPHABETICAL

LIST OF MEMBERS

—OF—

Petaluma Lodge, No. 30,

I. O. O. F.

NAMES.	When Admitted.	How Admitted	Rank
Atwater, Henry H	Jun 20, 1866	Initiation	P G
Anderson, F. A.	Feb 17, '85	Card	P G
Anderson, Hugh	Apr 23, '72	Initiation	3d Dg
Batman, James W	Aug 2, '65	Card	P G
Brown, William S	May 25, '80	Initiation	P G
Bauer, J. William	May 24, '81	Initiation	P G
Blackburn, Charles	Oct 15, '67	Initiation	3d Dg
Buckius, William L	May 18, '86	Initiation	1st Dg
Bradley, Walter Price	Mch 29, '87	Initiation	3d Dg
Branch, George Byron	Dec 17, '89	Initiation	3d Dg
Barnes, Jehu	May 16, '71	Initiation	3d Dg
Baur, John	Jun 17, '73	Initiation	3d Dg
Baltz, Charles	July 20, '75	Initiation	3d Dg
Blackburn, John S	Oct 26, '75	Initiation	3d Dg
Brady, Erwin	Apr 21, '63	Initiation	3d Dg
Bryant, Charles G	Feb 16, '69	Initiation	2d Dg
Barnes, Henry	Apr 28, '85	Initiation	3d Dg

NAMES.	When Admitted	How Admitted	Rank
Campbell, Joseph	Oct 19, 1869	Card	P G
Corliss, William B	Apr 16, '72	Initiation	P G
Cowen, Joseph A	Dec 4, '83	Initiation	P G
Congrove, J	July 18, '66	Initiation	3d Dg
Cushing, C. A	Nov 5, '67	Initiation	3d Dg
Coons, William W	May 19, '68	Initiation	3d Dg
Camm, William	Aug 1, '71	Initiation	3d Dg
Campigli, Charles	Aug 25, '74	Initiation	3d Dg
Canevascini, J. L	Feb 21, '82	Initiation	3d Dg
Colburn, C. E	Dec 2, '74	A O F	3d Dg
Clark, Byron	June 22, '75	Initiation	3d Dg
Cook, Isaac F	Dec 13, '7c	Card	3d Dg
Canepa, L	July 24, '83	Initiation	3d Dg
Cameron, Oliver P	July 19, '81	Initiation	3d Dg
Cadwell, J. A	May 15, '83	Initiation	3d Dg
Church, L. J	Oct 19, '8c	Initiation	3d Dg
Chaim, Henry	Feb 19, '89	Initiation	3d Dg
Crawford, Isaac S	Dec 17, '89	A O F	P G
Cowen, A. H	Feb 26, '84	Initiation	3d Dg
Cox, B. F	Dec 22, '68	Initiation	3d Dg
Dryden, C. C	May 13, '84	Card	P G
Drees, E. E	Oct 7, '84	Initiation	P G
Doyle, Frank P	Apr 13, '86	Initiation	P G
Densmore, John E	Dec 13, '7c	Initiation	3d Dg
Davis, Ira	Aug 22, '71	Initiation	3d Dg
Densmore, George F	Sept 2, '84	Initiation	3d Dg
Davis, E. W	Aug 18, '85	Initiation	3d Dg
Drees, Gustave A	Mch 2, '86	Initiation	3d Dg
Donogh, Andrew	Mch 25, '90	Initiation	3d Dg
Edelman, George W	Jan 28, '68	Initiation	P G
Elder, James W	Jun 20, '71	Initiation	P G
Ellsworth, Lee	Mch 13, '58	Initiation	P G

NAMES.	When Admitted	How Admitted	Rank
Ellsworth, Henry L	Jul 28, 1885	Initiation	P G
Effinger, C	Jan 9, '72	Card	3d Dg
Evans, Alex	Feb 15, '72	Initiation	3d Dg
Ennis, Frank F	Jul 23, '72	A O F	3d Dg
Edmeads, Edward	Dec 9, '84	Initiation	3d Dg
Fernald, Johnson	Jan 13, '64	Non- Affil	P G
Fritsch, John	Mch 3, '68	Initiation	P G
Fritsch, Walter S	June 1, '80	Initiation	P G
Fulmer, Joseph B	Jan 12, '75	Initiation	P G
Farrell, William F	Dec 12, '82	Initiation	P G
Frazier, L	May 11, '69	Initiation	3d Dg
Fine, Emsley	Jun 3, '90	Initiation	3d Dg
Freeman, W. D	May 23, '76	Initiation	3d Dg
Fritsch, J. R	Apr 3, '77	Initiation	3d Dg
Freeman, M. L	Jun 14, '81	Initiation	3d Dg
Frost, Walter J	May 3, '87	Initiation	3d Dg
Fox, Albert	Jan 7, '90	Card	3d Dg
Giacomini, Natale	Jan 26, '69	Initiation	3d Dg
Guttermute, Henry	Nov 16, 86	Initiation	3d Dg
Glover, Charles	Jan 31, '88	Card	3d Dg
Glenn, John C	Apr 23, '89	Initiation	3d Dg
Gist, John L	May 20, '90	Initiation	3d Dg
Gibbs; J. D	May 23, '76	Initiation	3d Dg
Gerckens, J. H. L	Mch 27, '77	Initiation	3d Dg
Green, G. D. Jr	Jan 22, '84	Initiation	3d Dg
Glenn, William	Oct 24, '76	Initiation	2d Dg
Harris, J. W	Mch 3, '58	Card	P G
Haskell, William B	Apr 21, '68	Initiation	P G
Hopkins, S. J	Apr 24, '77	Initiation	P G
Hopes, Edward	Jun 6, '66	Initiation	P G
Harris, William S	Feb 26, '84	Initiation	P G

NAMES.	When Admitted	How Admitted	Rank
Hopper, Thomas	Jun 30, 1855	Initiation	3d Dg
Hineberg, B	Aug 15, '66	A O F	3d Dg
Hemmenway, D. D	Dec 22, '68	Initiation	3d Dg
Haskins, Thomas J	Jun 6, '66	Initiation	3d Dg
Haskins, Robert	Feb 4, '73	Initiation	3d Dg
Hartleb, Fred	Sep 21, '69	Initiation	3d Dg
Hayne, W. H	Aug 15, '82	Initiation	3d Dg
Hedges, E. D	Jul 31, '83	Initiation	3d Dg
Heaney, Hugh	Mch 9, '86	Initiation	3d Dg
Harter, Bloomfield	Dec 22, '80	Initiation	3d Dg
Haskins, W. R	Jul 22, '84	Initiation	3d Dg
Ingwerson, W. H	Oct 29, '89	Initiation	3d Dg
Jenks, George H	Jul 23, '67	Initiation	P G
Johnson, John E	Mch 26, '78	Initiation	P G
Johnson, A. T	Feb 28, '66	Initiation	3d Dg
Jones, Robert	Mch 5, '78	Initiation	3d Dg
Jordan, H. H	Aug 22, '82	Initiation	3d Dg
Knowles, James H	May 30, '66	Initiation	P G
Kill, James M	Dec 2, '84	Initiation	P G
King, Charles	Jan 10, '71	Initiation	3d Dg
Knowles, W. H. F	Jan 21, '73	Card	3d Dg
Kuhnle, Fred	Oct 7, '73	Initiation	3d Dg
Kyle, Thomas	Oct 9, '83	Initiation	3d Dg
Lamoreaux, Geo. W	Mch 21, '71	Initiation	3d Dg
Lawlor, John	Jan 7, '79	Initiation	3d Dg
Lockwood, J. E. Jr	Jul 31, '83	Initiation	3d Dg
Light, Eugene	Nov 9, '69	Initiation	3d Dg
Lightner, John S	Nov 27, '77	Initiation	3d Dg
Lockwood, J. E. Sr	Aug 25, '68	Initiation	3d Dg
Lent, David A	Nov 11, '84	Initiation	3d Dg

NAMES.	When Admitted.	How Admitted	Rank
Lent, Alonza	Jun 22, 1886	Initiation	3d Dg
Lausen, Andrew	Jan 12, '75	Initiation	3d Dg
Martin, Silas M	Sep 30, '54	Initiation	P G
Meyerholtz, Henry	Jun 20, 71	Initiation	3d Dg
Mason, C. H	Dec 22, '60	Non-Affil	3d Dg
Matzenbach, W. B	Aug 29, '66	Card	3d Dg
Meyer, Anton	Jan 21, '68	Card	3d Dg
Myers, Frank H	Oct 29, '89	Initiation	3d Dg
Mitchell, Charles	Mch 29, '70	Initiation	3d Dg
Moen, G. O	Apr 29, '79	Initiation	3d Dg
Middagh, W. A	May 24, '81	Initiation	3d Dg
Mengel, Henry J	Mch 15, '81	Initiation	3d Dg
Maybee, John I. D	Mch 18, '84	Initiation	3d Dg
Maybee, Frank E	Mch 18, '84	Initiation	3d Dg
Meyer, J. F	Feb 17, '85	Card	P G
Moiles, Theo	Apr 22, '79	Initiation	3d Dg
McPhail, Andrew J	Apr 6, '86	Initiation	3d Dg
McDonald, John	May 10, '87	Initiation	3d Dg
McNair, D	Jan 9, '72	Initiation	3d Dg
McKay, A	July 11, '71	Initiation	3d Dg
McLennan, M K	Oct 14, '84	Initiation	3d Dg
Newburgh, Edward	Nov 26, '67	A O F	P G
Nay, L. G	Mch 3, '68	Initiation	P G
Nay, W. J	May 13, '73	Initiation	3d Dg
Nay, S. A	Aug 6, '73	Initiation	3d Dg
Newell, J. M	Sep 9, '74	Initiation	3d Dg
Northrup, Charles F	July 31, '83	Initiation	3d Dg
Nimmins, J	Jun 3, '90	Initiation	3d Dg
Naylor, Joseph	Mch 2, '86	Initiation	3d Dg
Nauert, Henry	Apr 13, '86	Initiation	3d Dg
Nauert, Fred A	Apr 13, '86	Initiation	3d Dg
Nickel, Albert P	Feb 10, '85	Initiation	3d Dg

NAMES.	When Admitted	How Admitted	Rank
Oster, Henry	Aug 15, 1882	Initiation	P G
O'Keefe, William	May 18, '64	Initiation	3d Dg
Ormsby, G. W	Aug 15, '71	Initiation	3d Dg
Pimm, Henry	Apr 21, '66	Initiation	P G
Putnam, D. W. C	May 16, '66	Non-Affil	P G
Poehlmann, Conrad	Sep 24, '67	Initiation	P G
Putnam, Charles S	May 18, '86	Initiation	3d Dg
Pimm, H. J	Apr 13, '86	Initiation	3d Dg
Peters, Prentice C	Apr 22, '90	Initiation	3d Dg
Pander, Henry	Oct 22, '72	Initiation	3d Dg
Peterson, Julius A	Jan 29, '78	Initiation	3d Dg
Poehlmann, Henry J	Mch 5, '78	Initiation	3d Dg
Phillips, Jacob	Jan 17, '66	Initiation	3d Dg
Perry, James S	Sep 11, '83	Initiation	3d Dg
Peters, Charles R	Sep 4, '83	Initiation	3d Dg
Perry, Earnest W	Feb 26, '84	Initiation	3d Dg
Penry, James F	Dec 25, '83	Card	3d Dg
Paff, George S	May 12, '85	Initiation	3d Dg
Powers, W. J	Aug 24, '69	Initiation	2d Dg
Pedrazzini, L	Mch 10, '68	Initiation	3d Dg
Rowlson, E	Sep 1, '60	Non–Affil	P G
Ross, David	Mch 27, '80	Initiation	P G
Reniff, Asa A	Feb 11, '68	Card	3d Dg
Ranard, J. M	Jun 21, '70	Initiation	3d Dg
Roberts, Samuel	Jul 20, '75	Initiation	3d Dg
Roberts, Hugh J	Aug 21, '81	Card	3d Dg
Rickert, I. F	Dec 29, '68	Initiation	3d Dg
Sackett, D. A	Dec, 31, '56	Card	P G
Sloper, Williard	Feb 15, '65	A O F	P G
Sproule, John	Sep 14, '69	Card	P G
St. John, S. C	Apr 3, '77	Initiation	P G

NAMES.	When Admitted	How Admitted	Rank
Spotswood, Geo. W...	Jul 31, '83	Initiation	P G
Spotswood, R. H.........	Oct 7, '84	Initiation	P G
Seavey, R............	Jan 12, '69	Non–Affil	3d Dg
Smith, Jos. G	Feb 16, '69	Initiation	3d Dg
Steitz, L. F....	Mch 19, '89	Initiation	3d Dg
Schleicker, Fred... ...	Jul 5, '70	Initiation	3d Dg
Sylvester, C. S............	Nov 29, '70	Initiation	3d Dg
Shaver, Simon............	Apr 2, '72	Initiation	3d Dg
Steiger, P. J...............	Aug11, '74	Initiation	3d Dg
Spotswood, Andrew....	Nov 6, '77	Initiation	3d Dg
Scott, Jas. F	Sep 30, '73	Initiation	3d Dg
Symonds, C. W	Mch 23, '69	Initiation	3d Dg
Stafford, E. P............	Jul 31, '83	Initiation	3d Dg
Shattuck, W. F...	Sep 11 '77	Initiation	3d Dg
Samuelson, J. P .	Nov 6, '83	Card 3d	Dg
Smith, Albert A......	Apr 9' 78	Initiation	3d Dg
Sinclair, Henry G	Jul 22, '90	Initiation	3d Dg
Toms, S. A............	Sep 11, '83	Initiation	P G
Tupper, J. B...............	Apr 29, '73	Initiation	3d Dg
Thurston, Andrew	Aug 6, '73	Initiation	3d Dg
Tomasini, Louis	Nov 13, '77	Initiation	3d Dg
Twist, Albert G	Jul 19, '81	Initiation	3d Dg
Tyler, John N....	Sep 4, '83	Initiation	3d Dg
Tyler, Albin N.............	Sep 30, '84	Initiation	3d Dg
Wiswell, Joseph A	Apr 18, '66	A O F...	P G
Weber, Martin.............	Nov 19, '76	Card	P G
Ward, Abram	Sep 8, '55	Initiation	P G
Weber, William N.....	Oct 16, '83	Card	P G
Weber, Jos. A.............	May 17, '87	Initiation	3d Dg
Walker, Geo. F............	Feb 23, '88	Initiation	3d Dg
Waddell, J. H	May 28, '89	Card	3d Dg
Wharff, David.............	Nov 24, '68	Initiation	3d Dg

NAMES.	When Admitted		How Admitted	Rank
Walls, David	May 2,	'71	Card	3d Dg
Woods, George	Oct 26,	'73	Card	3d Dg
Winans, David M.	May 20,	'73	Initiation	3d Dg
Weber, Martin J	Oct 16,	'83	Card	3d Dg
Winans, Louis J	Oct 24,	'84	Initiation	3d Dg
Wharff, N. P B	Jun 11,	'78	Initiation	3d Dg
Young, Chas. M	Apr 22,	'79	Card	P G
Young, Chas	Jul 25,	'76	Initiation	3d Dg
Young, Geo. C.	Jun 29,	'86	Initiation	3d Dg
Zartman, William H	Dec 29,	'55	Initiation	P G
Zartman, B. F	Jan 11,.	'76	Initiation	P G
Zartman, W	Jul 31,	'83	Initiation	3d Dg
Zamaroni, P	Sep 30,	'73	Initiation	3d Dg

Total number of Members 218

PETITION FOR MEMBERSHIP.

....*18*....

To the N. G., V. G., Officers and Members of
...........................*Lodge, No*......, *I. O. O. F.*

*GENTLEMEN.—Entertaining a favorable
opinion of your Benevolent Order, I am desirous
of becoming a member thereof, and of admission
into your Lodge; and if elected will cheerfully
conform to your Constitution, By-Laws, Rules and
Regulations.*

My residence is...

Age................*Occupation*................................

I was born in..

Health good.

Signature of Applicant..................................

Recommended by...

Refers to $\left\{ \begin{array}{l} .... \\ .... \end{array} \right.$

PETITION BY DEPOSIT OF CARD.

———

To the N. G., V. G., Officers and Brothers

of ....Lodge, No... ....I. O. O. F.

BRETHERN:—Herewith I present my card of

Withdrawal from..............Lodge, No...I. O. O. F.,

of..............and respectfully ask to be admitted a

member of your Lodge by deposit of the same.

My age is.............. ....Occupation...... ......

Residence ....I was born in ....

Health, good.

Fraternally yours, in F. L. and T.,

....

Proposed and Recommended by—

....

Refers to {
....
....

ORDER OF PROCESSION.

Music.

Marshal.

Outside Sentinel.
(With Drawn Sword.)

Escort. Banner Escort.

Scene Supporters.
(Bearing White Wands.)

Initiatory, First, Second and Third Degree

Members.
(Two or four abreast.)

Past Grands.
(In Order of Juniority.)

Inside Guardian.
(With Drawn Sword.)

Conductor. Chaplain. Warden
(Bearing Wand.) (With White Scarf.) (Bearing Axe.)

Secretary. Treasurer. Secretary.

Supporter. Vice Grand. Supporter.
(Bearing Wand of Office.) (Bearing Wand of Office.)

Supporter. Noble Grand. Supporter.
(Bearing Wand.) (With Gavel.) (Bearing Wand.)

Upon arriving at the place of destination, the procession will halt and open to the right and left, until they come to the Noble Grand, who will pass between the two lines when they will close in the rear and follow.

INDEX.